Working with Children with Specific Learning Difficulties in the Early Years

by
Dorothy Smith

A QEd Publication

Published in 2001

ISBN 1 898873 18 6

Published by QEd, The Rom Building, Eastern Avenue, Lichfield, Staffordshire WS13 6RN
Website: www.qed.uk.com
Email: orders@qed.uk.com

Typeset by J. C. Typesetting.
Printed in the United Kingdom by Stowes (Stoke-on-Trent).

Contents

Introduction

Early years education is termed the Foundation Stage and this includes children from the age of 3 to the end of their reception year. There is, therefore, an overlap between children attending pre-school settings and their compulsory attendance at school which is the beginning of the term after their fifth birthday. The Foundation Stage is a preparation for working within Key Stage 1.

Curriculum guidance for the foundation stage (QCA/DfEE, May 2000) uses the term 'practitioners' for those adults who work within early years settings. This book will use the words teachers, educators, adults and supporters. The word parent is used as the generic term for those who are the primary carers.

It should be stressed that this book is not intended to be a definitive guide for identifying and *labelling* early years children as having specific learning difficulties but as an aid for all who work with young children to observe their strengths and weaknesses and provide appropriate programmes and activities if these are felt necessary. As is stressed throughout the book many observable features within children's learning in the early years may be the result of developmental delay (or maturation) and need not necessarily be signs of specific learning difficulties. Many of the activities or programmes suggested are those which can be used for *all* children and not just for those who are causing any concern.

Chapter 1
Background information

'Specific learning difficulties' is an umbrella term which is used to describe the special educational needs of a group of children who have particular learning problems. The 'specific' nature of the special educational need indicates that the child's learning problems do not show themselves in every area of the curriculum, rather that they affect only certain aspects of learning, mostly those which require literacy acquisition. Within the *SEN Code of Practice on the Identification and Assessment of Pupils with Special Educational Needs* and the *SEN Thresholds: Good Practice Guidance on Identification and Provision for Pupils with Special Educational Needs*, Draft Code and Guidance (DfEE, July 2000) specific learning difficulties is set within the section Cognition and Learning, whereas within the *Code of Practice* (DfE, 1994), it is one of the eight described categories of special educational need.

Included within the broad term are other labels which are used to describe children who have specific learning difficulties. The more common of these are dyslexia and dyspraxia. Because of the specific nature of the learning need there are other categories of special educational need which can also be linked with the overall umbrella term, such as dyscalculia, dysphasia, ADD (attention deficit disorder) and ADHD (attention deficit hyperactivity disorder) and high level functioning autism and Asperger's syndrome.

A brief history

At the end of the nineteenth century members of the medical profession were beginning to describe certain individuals as 'word blind', a label which later changed to 'dyslexic'. It was noted that despite seemingly average intelligence some children were unable to make sense of the printed word for reading and to cope with spelling. The similarity in their problems were that the children appeared to find it difficult to cope with visual recognition and orientation of letters and with letter order in words. One of the many terms for this 'condition' was 'strephosymbolia' which meant 'twisted symbols'. There were many such terms and an early one included the now-used term 'specific' as in 'specific language disability'. The term 'dyslexia' appears to have been given around the 1930s when members of the educational profession started devising specialised teaching methods.

5

Dyslexia was very much the province of the medical profession in the first half of the twentieth century and even in 1970 when The Chronically Sick and Disabled Persons Act was passed there was reference to the term 'acute dyslexia'. By 1972 dyslexia started to enter public awareness and the BDA (The British Dyslexia Association) was founded. In 1981 the Warnock Report made specific learning difficulties one of its four broad bands of special educational need and the Education Act 1981 recognised that some children have special educational needs and that these children needed accurate assessment and probably different types of teaching. The present draft Code (2000) continues to use the term 'specific learning difficulties' although the terms 'dyslexia' and 'dyspraxia' are used in paragraph 7.16 – which perhaps indicates that it is recognised that these words are generally better known by the general public than the umbrella term.

Much research has taken place in recent years to try to determine the particular problems experienced by children with dyslexia. The word literally means 'difficulty with words' and is derived from the Greek as are so many medical terms. Educationists and researchers have spent a great deal of time investigating the way children learn and their particular problems with the written word. Much of this research has centred upon the auditory side to language learning and the difficulties children experience with phonological awareness and usage. However, recently there has been some additional research undertaken into the visual side to specific learning difficulties.

What are specific learning difficulties?

There are many definitions of dyslexia, fewer of the term specific learning difficulties, and they are all broadly similar. Children with a specific learning difficulty have a developmental problem and one that is constitutional in origin with evidence that there is a heritable factor. There are some cases of acquired dyslexia where problems with reading and spelling occur because of brain injuries usually in an accident but the vast majority of children with specific learning difficulties are born with the difficulties or the difficulties are seen to develop as the children grow older and learning becomes more demanding. Problems occur because of particular visual and/or auditory processing and memory difficulties which can affect working with words, in language, reading and spelling, and sometimes with numbers. However, not just literacy and perhaps numeracy are affected. The individual may also have additional spatial and motor problems which have implications for other areas of learning.

The *Code of Practice*, 1994, gives a definition of specific learning difficulties as:

'Some children may have significant difficulties in reading, writing, spelling or manipulating number, which are not typical of their general level of performance. They may gain some skills in some subjects quickly and demonstrate a high level of ability orally, yet may encounter sustained difficulty in gaining literacy or numeracy skills. Such children can become severely frustrated and may also have emotional and/or behavioural difficulties.'

(Code of Practice, 1994, para. 3:60)

This Code continues by listing other components which need to be recorded in order to show that a child has specific learning difficulties. The first two of these look into discrepancies between attainment and ability; the fourth reiterates the frustrational aspect and lack of self-esteem which might occur whilst the third adds some additional factors:

'There is clear, recorded evidence of clumsiness; significant difficulties of sequencing or visual perception; deficiencies in working memory; or significant delays in language functioning.'

(Code of Practice, 1994, para. 3.61)

These four sections (plus others) are found in the *SEN Code of Practice on the Identification and Assessment of Pupils with Special Educational Needs* (Draft Code, July 2000) under the general section pertaining to Statutory Assessment (para. 7.12) whereas in the *SEN Thresholds: Good Practice Guidance on Identification and Provision for Pupils with Special Educational Needs* attached to the *SEN Code of Practice on the Identification and Assessment of Pupils with Special Educational Needs* (Draft, July 2000) the definition has been replaced by a set of factors which might be present in a child who is described as having specific learning difficulties.

These cover the following:

• difficulties within the areas of motor skills, both gross and fine;

• low attainment in one or more curriculum areas, in particular because of difficulties in literacy and/or numeracy skills;

- evidence that the learning difficulties are not over the whole curriculum and will show where certain areas of the curriculum present higher attainment than others;
- signs of frustration and/or low self-esteem which may be shown in behavioural problems;
- particular difficulties in specific areas such as sequencing, organisation, short-term memory and with phonological abilities;
- language difficulties such as expressive problems and delays in forming concepts particularly where younger children are concerned.

Early definitions of dyslexia were based around reading problems whereas more recent ones are far broader. The BDA description states:

'Dyslexia is best described as a combination of abilities and difficulties which affect the learning process in one or more of reading, spelling, writing and sometimes numeracy/language. Accompanying weaknesses may be identified in areas of speed of processing, short-term memory, sequencing, auditory and/or visual perception, spoken language and motor skills.

Some children have outstanding creative skills, others have strong oral skills. Whilst others have no outstanding talents they all have strengths.

Dyslexia occurs despite normal intellectual ability and conventional teaching; it is independent of socio-economic or language background.'
(*The Dyslexia Handbook 2000*, p.67)

There are definitions for the other labels which have been referred to. Again there are similarities between them which indicates the specificity of the specific learning difficulty although in each of them a particular focus is emphasised. Dyspraxia is a dysfunction of co-ordination where the child has difficulties with acquiring patterns of movement, with efficiency of co-ordination. It shows itself in poor spatial awareness and problems with handwriting and other fine motor control activities. Some children have gross motor difficulties and others have problems with the muscles which co-ordinate the movement needed for speech and consequently their speech is unclear and inefficient. These children have verbal and/or articulatory dyspraxia. Dyspraxia is a developmental disorder and one that occurs when parts of the brain have failed to mature correctly. One definition of dyspraxia states:

'Dyspraxia is an impairment or immaturity of the organisation of movement. Associated with this there may be problems of language, perception and thought.'

(*Information for Parents*, the Dyspraxia Foundation)

Dyscalculia is the specific problem with the acquisition of numeracy, and dysphasia is a specific language problem rather than one of articulation. This language problem can affect receptive language skills, the understanding of words and how they are used, and expressive language which is the way words are used to convey meaning. ADD (Attention Deficit Disorder) and ADHD (Attention Deficit Hyperactive Disorder) are specific problems affecting concentration and maintaining attention. There can be additional impulsivity of behaviour. ASD (Autistic Spectrum Disorder) is a particular difficulty concerned with a triad of impairments in the areas of language and social communication, social relationships and imaginative thought.

It can be recognised that there are possible relationships within all the above categories of learning difficulty which bring them under the specific learning difficulties umbrella. As a general rule it is the child's working memory, visual and/or auditory, that is the key problem. The working memory is most important within the process of learning. It is the part of the memory function that has to retain any input collected from the senses (either visual and/or auditory) which can be immediate or brought back from long-term memory. This input or information has to be understood and then organised and this is usually a sequential process before it is put to use and acted upon in some form and then returned to the long-term memory store. Therefore, if the working memory is weak then any process which requires its use, such as reading, spelling, mathematics and self-organisation, will be impaired and faulty.

An example of this could be learning a nursery rhyme where:

• the words are heard and repeated (as many times as is necessary) and assimilated into the long-term memory bank;

• the words should be understood so that correct repetition occurs;

9

- the words have to be sequenced correctly;
- at another time when the title of the nursery rhyme is given this should trigger the memory store;
- the words are then brought to the working memory and organised;
- the rhyme is recited.

If a child has a weak working memory there may be difficulties with the initial repetition and acquisition of the words. Words may be mispronounced because of poor understanding. They might be muddled especially if there is little understanding of the use of rhyme at the end of the lines. The title may not trigger past learning and the nursery rhyme will be recited in part or not at all.

Any definitions are, of course, broad and necessarily have to cover all eventualities. A model which can help to explain specific learning difficulties is one that divides into three areas. The first is the biological where theories concerning hereditary and the brain are explored, which can be labelled as the *emotional/biological* level. The second is concerned with the learning processing, the auditory, visual and motor processes required for efficient learning to take place. This is the *cognitive* level. The third contains what can be observed as the child reads, spells, writes, in fact learns, within the educational environment and outside. This is the *behavioural* level. These levels are interdependent. But as will be covered later, the allocation of such labels, any theories that abound and the models that are given tell us little about the learning needs of any individual child. Detailed observation is required.

Chapter 2
Developing and implementing procedures for the regular observation and assessment of children

Although the *Code of Practice*, 1994, emphasised early identification of children's special educational needs it has not been usual over the past years to label children in the early years as having specific learning difficulties or being dyslexic. However, the revised Code pursues this theme of early identification and states:

'The importance of early identification, assessment and provision for any child who may have special educational needs cannot be overemphasised. The earlier action is taken, the more responsive the child is likely to be, and the more readily can intervention be made without undue disruption to the organisation of the school. Assessment should not be regarded as a single event but rather as a continuing process.'

(*Code of Practice,* Draft 2000, para. 5.2)

It is important to initiate ongoing observation of all children and this is usually well organised within early years settings. In whatever way the observation takes place and whatever is observed and noted, teachers and early years educators must be wary of labelling at too early an age. As will become apparent there are indicators of specific learning difficulties which are also developmental or maturational factors. But even if this is so it can still be helpful for learning programmes to be put into place once a weakness has been pinpointed. It is the *severity* of the perceived problem and the *length of time* it persists that is significant. *Clarity* of *recording* the difficulties is also very important.

When specific learning difficulties was seen only as a dyslexic problem which related solely to learning to read and spell then it was felt that 6 years of age was the earliest that a child could be labelled. It was at this age that early skills of reading and writing, including spelling, either had made progress or problems were being perceived. With more recent concepts about the factors seen within children with specific learning difficulties early identification, even before statutory school age, can be beneficial, as long as the information is used constructively. This will be dealt with in Chapter 3 when learning activities are discussed.

The BDA in *The Dyslexia Handbook 1997* gives a list of signs which can be a useful guide although the way they are set out is very general rather than being subdivided into more detailed areas. These give a section on strengths and then pointers under two headings, 'general' and 'speech and language'. The former is important because one should not just dwell on the negative but on the positive as well. Because one of the differences between specific and general learning difficulties concerns the notion of intelligence, the way the child with specific learning difficulties has a skewed learning profile, it is necessary to state what this child can do well.

Strengths

- quick 'thinker' and 'doer' – but not in response to instructions;
- enhanced creativity – often good at drawing – good sense of colour;
- aptitude for constructional or technical toys, e.g. bricks, puzzles, Lego, blocks, remote control for TV and/or video, computer keyboard;
- appears bright – but seems an enigma.

(*The Dyslexia Handbook,* 1997, p. 67)

It is interesting to see that the above might not take into account that some children with specific learning difficulties could have spatial problems which would make constructional and technical activities difficult. Nor does it look at the child with dyspraxic problems, with difficulties in the area of fine motor skills, who would find drawing and working with toys such as Lego difficult activities.

These strengths look at the probable cognitive learning factors, the intelligence level. Although educational psychologists have assessments which can purport to measure the intelligence of young children, any such procedure is not necessarily accurate and there will be very few young children for whom it will be felt necessary to undertake such a testing procedure. Undertaking intelligence tests such as the BAS (British Abilities Scale) and WPPSI-R (Weschler Pre-school and Primary Scale of Intelligence) can be time-consuming and, because young children may have short concentration spans, they can be difficult to administer in one session. Therefore, there is the requirement for adults, educators, other supporters and parents to use their judgements. Although these may be subjective they can be supported by additional statements such as 'appears bright because he asks many questions about the origins of the world and seems to be very interested in the answers' or 'appears bright as she copes well with the practical activities within the Home Corner and can organise these, having obviously well learnt routines'.

Another set of statements for looking at children's abilities can be found in *Living With Dyslexia* (Riddick, 1996). Riddick questioned a group of mothers and placed the qualities they mentioned about their child under three general headings. These, she explained, were somewhat arbitrary as some of the items could be placed under more than one heading. These headings were 'good abstract reasoning', 'good memory and language skills' and 'intelligent practical skills and interest in learning'. The first which is concerned with the child's ability to work in the abstract and to be perceptive and part of the second which mentions good language skills indicate that some parents did not see language acquisition and usage as being a problem although as already stated, the *Code of Practice* mentions that there could be problems in this area for children with specific learning difficulties. It is also interesting that some of these mothers felt that although their child was dyslexic they had good long-term memory skills. However, what is of importance in Riddick's study is that the mothers had been aware of their children as being *learning different* and many of them felt they identified the particular problem within the pre-school setting.

Regardless of what constitutes a 'bright' or intelligent child as measured by psychometric tests the information that the parents can give, backed up by what the workers in early years settings can observe, will give some valuable insight to the child's learning styles and competencies.

Areas of possible concern

Working from a checklist giving indicators for parents and professionals who have involvement with early years children, although helpful, is fraught with problems. As has already been mentioned these pointers contain factors which can be found in the general course of learning in most children. Therefore, one has to be aware of when an apparent weakness might be developmental and routine and when it might cause concern. What is of particular importance is to make sure that *all* early years children in whatever setting develop the mastery of certain 'early learning' skills if they are going to be able to learn to read and write successfully and to cope with later school life.

13

However, it is still important to use observational techniques during the everyday activities of the children in order to ascertain where there are strengths and where the child might be having difficulties or maybe potential difficulties. Working with parents to find out their views is important as children react differently in different situations. As the revised Code states:

'Parents hold key information and have a critical role to play in their child's education. If they feel confident that schools and professionals involve them, take account of their wishes, feelings and unique perspectives on their child's development, then the work of those schools and professionals can be more effective.'

(Code of Practice, Draft 2000, para. 2.1)

Familial similarities

One area where parents alone can give an answer is the question of hereditary problems. Some parents who are well aware of a familial difficulty may be concerned that their child might also have the same type of problem and so will be alert to any similar difficulties the child might show. Other parents may only recall family members with specific learning difficulties or what they will probably call dyslexia when asked by the educationist and this will only occur when the identification process has started. There are, of course, those parents who feel guilty or ashamed that they might have passed on their specific learning problem to their child and may deny the hereditary suggestion. Although, currently, dyslexia has become an openly talked about problem with many people in the media (such as those concerned with creative arts, acting, sport and entrepreneurial pursuits) happy to discuss how they have overcome their dyslexia, there are still many 'ordinary' men and women who do not have the same confidence about the subject. Sympathetic and careful communication needs to take place in these instances.

The importance of early identification

The revised Code contains a chapter devoted to Identification, Assessment and Provision in Early Years Settings indicating that DfEE stresses the importance of early identification. Wherever the early education is provided is part of what is termed the Foundation Stage of education, where children experience 'rapid physical, emotional, intellectual and social growth'. The Government sets out achievable targets within the Early Learning Goals which represent the expected outcomes of education that combines both play and learning. Those children who do not meet the expectations may be

14

developmentally delayed especially if they are younger, that is summer born children who have received less time in the particular educational setting. Or they may have special educational needs within certain broad categories. The importance of good observational techniques may help decide upon explanations for the apparent weaknesses.

The revised Code states:

'Practitioners should work closely with parents to build on children's previous experiences, knowledge, understanding and skills ...'

(Code of Practice, Draft 2000, para. 4.2)

It indicates that there are certain areas of children's learning which should develop during the Foundation Stage and it will be within these areas that observation will take place. The *Curriculum guidance for the foundation stage* (QCA/DfEE, May 2000) states that:

'Practitioners must be able to observe and respond appropriately to children, informed by a knowledge of how children develop and learn and a clear understanding of possible next steps in their development and learning.'

(p. 11)

These broad areas can be looked at more closely where possible specific learning difficulties are concerned. 'Knowledge and understanding of the world' might indicate the child's possible cognitive ability. 'Physical development' and 'creative development' may verify strengths but as already mentioned problems in these areas might be due to problems of motor skills. 'Mathematical development' and 'Communication, language and literacy' links with specific or dyslexic problems and 'Personal, social and emotional development' can be of importance when showing how children both relate to each other and how they can cope with perceived failure or difficulties. However, it is probable that children do not start to compare themselves with their peers until more 'formal' learning takes place, especially in the case of reading where it is readily apparent when a child has particular difficulties.

There are certain areas that can be checked by ongoing observational recording which are connected with the definitions of specific learning difficulties and its related terminology. There is no way one can substantiate that a certain number of positive pointers can categorically determine that

15

the child has specific learning difficulties but each area of difficulty should lead to some action. Because of the connection with literacy and language attainment most of the examples given later will be about words but it should also be remembered that the acquisition of mathematical concepts is similar. Learning what numbers are, the process of counting, one-to-one correspondence, simple addition and other computation, writing and recording numbers, learning about shapes etc. require competent visual and auditory skills plus adequate fine motor control.

Language and general understanding

This sub-heading takes in two main areas and two others which connect with these and each can build up a picture of a child's development in the language areas. However, adults might discover that it is difficult to work on their findings because of the differences in data within the research on specific learning difficulties. As has been noted in Chapter 1 children with specific learning difficulties might have competent or even good oral skills or they might have particular difficulties within the areas of language acquisition, with delayed speech, poor articulation and weak language development.

Receptive language

This is the bank of words that a child understands. It contains all types of vocabulary from basic nouns through to more abstract concepts. From birth children hear speech and have to make sense of this. They may start by generalising that all animals are 'cats' or all men are 'daddy', for example. As they grow older they learn to discriminate and particularise. They change from understanding the term used at home for particular objects into acquiring the correct terminology. They learn prepositions, adjectives and adverbs alongside nouns and verbs and they begin to be aware that words might have two meanings depending on the context in which they are used. They learn to use the past and the future tenses instead of just using the present. Young children probably understand more than they speak, but adults when listening to words that the children use and questions that they ask can gain some idea of the amount of received vocabulary the children have internalised.

Adults can also assess a child's understanding by the way the child responds to instructions. These should be kept short because of possible problems with the child's auditory memory and one is just wanting to judge receptive language knowledge. Requests such as 'bring me the

16

orange crayon' and 'show me a green hoop' can assess knowledge of colours. When books are shared the child can be asked to point to certain items in the pictures. The names of everyday objects can be checked similarly in the shop or home corner. Knowledge of prepositions can be confirmed by asking the child to 'put the box under the table' or 'sit teddy behind the car'. Parents can easily be involved with these activities.

Checksheets can be made for everyday use so that the adults can make a note of what is seen to be understood and what words are causing difficulties. It is sensible to note on more than one occasion in order to make sure the knowledge is thoroughly internalised and is part of the child's long-term memory store. Because language is in use all day and every day nothing has to be set up out of the ordinary for observing and checking receptive language knowledge.

Expressive language

Expressive language, the use of language, is the logical follow-on to understanding language. Very young children use single words to make themselves understood and as they grow older use simple sentences and then more complicated ones with a range of vocabulary from simple words to more sophisticated speech. Parents can be asked if their child's language was late to develop. However, if the child was their first, parents may not always be able to compare their child's language development with that of others.

There are two parts of expressive language. One is articulation and the other is word usage. There is an order of acquired letter sounds (single sounds and letter combinations) which speech and language therapists refer to when assessing children whose articulatory speech is felt to be particularly poor or even unintelligible. Often children in the early years find the 'r' sound difficult to pronounce, many use a 'l' sound for an initial 'y' and 'f' for 'th'. It is the continuing and unusual difficulty that will be observed by the staff in the early years settings and advice can be obtained from speech and language therapists.

As with receptive language the child's use of vocabulary can be checked without any specialised organisation. Children need to be given time to answer questions whether these are direct ones such as 'what colour coat is the man wearing?' which require a one word answer or more complicated ones such as 'why do you think the girl is carrying an umbrella?' Time is

17

required in case the children have memory problems so they will need 'thinking time' before being expected to answer. There are two types of questions which can be used. Closed questions require a correct answer. These can be 'yes' or 'no' or a particular use of vocabulary. For example, if prepositions are being checked the adult might put a toy car under a piece of paper and ask the child 'where is the car'. The child might just want to point so encouragement should be given for a verbal response. Open questions require replies which can be of one's own judgement. There is no particular right or wrong answer and the child can be asked to justify why a particular response has been given. Children should also be given time to talk to adults, to tell them what they did on their birthday, what it was like at the zoo, what they watched on television etc. If this occurs not only can the adults listen to the range of vocabulary used and the language patterns but they can also ask questions and move the conversation on.

Some children with specific learning difficulties sometimes find it hard to recall particular words. They appear to know the concept or meaning of the word but cannot recall the label. They then use an alternative which is not quite correct. For example, the child might be describing the 'ground' but this word eludes the memory. The child then substitutes 'floor' which has a similar meaning but not within the context of out-of-doors. The sentence 'the flowers are growing in the floor' gives the impression of limited vocabulary knowledge whereas it might mean processing difficulties. They might also muddle words of time saying things such as 'I went to Tom's birthday party tomorrow' which leaves the listener wondering whether this event has happened or is about to happen.

Another recognised difficulty some children with specific learning difficulties can have is the tendency to make words into Spoonerisms and hear nothing wrong with this. The child might talk about a 'better lox' for a 'letter box' or say 'I've got a pig ben' for 'I've got a big pen'. Yet another language difficulty is that some children find it hard to sequence and order words within their speech. As with Spoonerisms they tend not to know that they have muddled up the word order. They might say 'My cat's had kittens little' or 'My sister baby is naughty.' A fourth problem links with phonological awareness and is the difficulty with pronouncing multi-syllabic words. One would not expect very young children to pronounce strange words and many young children might pronounce 'shoulder' as 'soldier' but some children certainly find some longer words beyond their capabilities.

With these four areas of difficulty it is necessary to see if they persist, for one or two examples do not constitute a specific problem.

Understanding and carrying out spoken instructions

This is linked with receptive language and here the child is required to process what the adult says, which is to internalise and make sense of it. Again this is dependent upon the child's auditory memory store because if the instruction is too long part of it will be forgotten. Therefore, if children do not carry out the instruction given the adult might think they have not understood the message, either the vocabulary or the concepts, whereas if the instruction was broken down all would be easily understood. Parents often wonder if their children understand when there is no reaction to commands. There are, of course, other reasons than understanding or memory problems why children do not want to respond to things at home. They might be in the middle of something which is far more important for them and they choose to 'selectively hear'. This can also happen in early years settings and adults must make sure they have the child's attention focused before giving instructions.

As already mentioned, one of the strengths mentioned by the BDA is 'a quick thinker and doer' but this is qualified by 'but not in response to instructions' which indicates that the understanding is within an acceptable range but there are auditory memory problems or speed of processing problems.

Organising and processing thoughts in order to express needs, to ask questions and to show interest in the world around them

This is linked with expressive language and connects again with the earlier mention of strengths in the language areas. The organisation and processing of thoughts is linked with auditory memory but the questioning aspect and the showing of interest could be seen to be connected to cognitive abilities. These show the conception of 'appears bright' suggested by the BDA. Any observations within this area will be subjective but annotated notes will back up feelings.

As mentioned in Chapter 1 there are some specific learning difficulties traits observed in children who are labelled as autistic or as having Asperger's syndrome. If there is great concern about a child's awareness and use of language, especially in the social communication and imaginative thought areas, coupled with additional problems with social relationships then advice should be requested from those with expertise in this area.

Visual areas

It is very important for children to have well-developed or well-developing visual approaches to aid learning. Competent visual abilities are particularly important for later reading and spelling acquisition but they also have implications for all areas of learning and for coping with daily living. There are five subsections within this area which intertwine. Eyesight problems which require corrective glasses are not dealt with in this section. Any child who might have sight problems should be seen by an optician.

All observations can occur during the day-by-day organisation of the settings but the adults may wish to concentrate on one particular area for a certain length of time and structure activities around it. Activities will need to be revisited to see whether any problems within the areas might have been due to developmental processes.

Visual perception

This is what the child actually sees. It requires the ability to look at detail. At a basic stage when children look at pictures they have to look carefully to see the details. There are many books that encourage children to see hidden objects. They have to look very deliberately and find things that might not be expected. A cow might have six legs so the child has to know the number of legs a cow should have and then work out whether the picture is correct. What the child sees on a page of writing is of great importance.

There is a condition termed Irlen Syndrome or Scotopic Sensitivity Syndrome (SSS) which is found in some individuals with specific learning difficulties. In basic terms it is the individual's ability to process spectral light, to cope with the coloured lights within white light. If they have problems in this area there can be difficulties with perceiving print on the page. Black letters on bright white pages can be distorted; letters move or become blurred. The white pages shine and the individual's eyes water – making processing print an uncomfortable process. Often this problem is only seen when print is small and closely packed on the page but some young children can show that they have SSS symptoms. These children prefer coloured backgrounds to pages in books; they reject white pages. If they look at books with white backgrounds their eyes may water and they might rub their eyes. If adults suspect that the child's perception is being impeded because of Irlen Syndrome they should contact those who can screen for the problem. Children with this problem may be helped by taking away the white backgrounds to pages and providing coloured backgrounds, or by being supplied with particular coloured overlays which will make looking at print easier and more comfortable. Clearly, if a child cannot perceive print with ease, then reading will not be an easy process to acquire.

Visual discrimination

Here the child has to be able to see differences between objects and later words, letters and numbers. It is very important for later reading and writing that children are able to distinguish between similar objects. There are many workbooks that contain rows of objects that are mostly similar but one is slightly different. There may be teddy bears with scarves. One will not have a scarf and the child has to find the different one. There are activities that can take place either in or out of the early years setting. Walking down the street can enable the child to look carefully at the cars, looking at colours, looking at shapes etc. Sameness and difference can be worked on in a variety of circumstances.

For young children their teddies are teddies whether they are held upside down or seen back to front. Similarly when they see a cup it does not matter how this is held, what colour it is, what size it is. It is still a cup. However, once a child has to learn a number or a letter name it is very important that the letter or number is seen and recognised in a particular way. It is very easy to muddle letters of similar shape, such as 'u/n', 'b/d/p', 'w/m' or the number '9' with 'p'. Other letters can be seen backwards and then written backwards such as 'l/t/f/s'. It must be realised that muddling such letters and numbers in sight recognition and writing is a problem experienced by most children when learning their letters and numbers. As with other incorrect approaches to learning it is the *extent* and *length* of the visual discrimination confusion that is important.

Visual sequencing

This is the ability to perceive letters and words in the correct order and is a later skill for reading and spelling. Although many children in the early years settings do not learn to read and spell it is still important for adults to realise that being able to see and retain letters in the correct order is important. Similarly this is a skill which is necessary for auditorially learning telephone numbers as adults often want early years children to learn their own phone number. Sequencing using pictures is a helpful activity where the child is given a set of pictures which tell a story as long as they are placed in the correct order. This activity can be linked with expressive language as the child has to tell the story using the picture clues.

Visual categorisation

At a general level children should be able to see the 'sameness' of objects and at a later stage they will need knowledge of visual similarities between words and letters. In this area children need to realise that although there are differences in the way things are made, drawn and written they can actually have the same name. Very young children learn to realise that their drinking cup serves the same purpose as the cup their parents use for drinking coffee and the same as the toy cup which they use in their games. Also they can work on sets of objects where they find things of the same shape or colour or objects which are used in the kitchen or in the garage.

Once they can see visual similarities in larger and more familiar objects they will find it easier when they see words such as 'house' and 'horse' and 'father' and 'fatter' where the words have only one different letter or when they start to learn words with the same initial letters such as 'Janet', 'Jane', 'Jack' and 'Jaswant' or words with the same visual patterns such as 'coat/boat/goat/stoat'.

Visual memory

In order to cope with the later skills of reading and spelling children need to have a competent visual memory. Words for reading have to be recognised as a whole shape, their names learnt and then recalled verbally. Words for spelling have also to be remembered as a whole shape, with the letters in the correct sequence and then written from memory. In order to gain visual memory skills children need to recall non-symbolic objects first. Too often young children watch television or videos without taking in detail. They gather an overall impression but when questioned about a colour someone was wearing, an animal that appeared etc. often they cannot bring this to mind. Adults can become aware of this within the early years setting when they ask particular questions about pictures they have shown or about something that happened in Assembly and there are those children who cannot recall and answer.

Auditory areas

It is also very important for children to have well-developed or well-developing auditory skills to aid learning. Competent auditory abilities are also important for later reading and spelling acquisition and, like visual skills, they also have implications for all areas of learning and for coping with daily living. There are six subsections within this area which intertwine. Hearing problems affect fine discrimination of sounds. Many children have hearing that fluctuates especially in the winter months because their ears become full of wax. Some young children's 'glue ear' problems become so great that they are fitted with grommets to help their loss of hearing. It is important that early years educators and parents liaise so that any lapse in hearing is accounted for and dealt with where necessary.

Again all observations can occur during the day-by-day organisation of the settings and as with visual skills the adults may wish to concentrate on one particular area for a certain length of time and structure activities around it. Activities will need to be revisited to see whether any problems within the areas might have been due to developmental processes or fluctuating hearing loss.

Auditory perception
This is the child's ability to hear sounds. This is quite straightforward as it is concerned with actual hearing and as already stated if there are any problems here they could be due to fluctuating hearing loss or problems with one ear so that sounds are only filtered in at one side. Some children seem to have 'selective hearing' in that they select when they want to hear and react. Often this is because they are doing something interesting and, therefore, do not want to change the activity or it could be that they really become engrossed with an activity and genuinely switch off from what is happening around them. Adults should note the circumstances when a child appears not to be hearing. Often children have to be focused into listening by the adult making eye contact or using their names.

Auditory discrimination
This follows on from auditory perception and is about how the child is able to hear differences in sounds. Again this can be affected by fluctuating hearing loss. Children need to be able to hear that words or letters are the same or different if they are later going to be able to cope with literacy. Before they work on fine discriminatory skills they can be observed listening to loud or soft sounds, to high or low sounds, to more than one sound at a time or single sounds. Here observation in musical activities would be very helpful. Although it is less common than visual discrimination difficulties there are some children with specific learning difficulties who confuse the sounds of the letters 'b/d/p' as well as visually confusing them. There are also certain letters with high frequency sounds such as 'd/t' which are easily confused and certain vowel sounds, 'a/u' and 'e/i' which are also difficult where auditory discrimination is concerned.

Auditory sequencing

When listening to oral speech or when read to and when reading for oneself the child has to possess the ability to hear letters and words in the correct order and, of course, to retain these which will come under the auditory memory skill. This is linked with expressive language and an awareness of word order within speech. If children can guess what might come next in a spoken sentence they may find it easier to read contextually when they are older, to be able to substitute a contextually correct word for one that is not immediately sight recognised. Another problem area within auditory sequencing which is linked with auditory memory problems is being able to give telephone numbers in their correct sequence, to know the days of the week, the months of the year or the alphabet with all items correctly recited.

Auditory categorisation

This links with auditory discrimination as the child needs a knowledge of similarities between the sounds of words and letters. They need to be able to realise that words can start with the same letter or that they can sound the same as in rhymes.

Auditory memory

Much of what a child has to do both at home and in the early years setting is bound up with hearing and remembering and then acting on what has been recalled. A great deal of what everyone does requires competent auditory memory skills. The working memory has already been discussed and it is this bridge between short-term and long-term memories and vice-versa that can cause specific learning difficulties to occur.

Within any group of children there might be some who appear to lack concentration, have problems with maintaining attention and 'stickability'. They might be restless, leaving activities before finishing them, or they might be impulsive, calling out without waiting their turn. It could be that these children have auditory memory problems so that they forget what they should be doing, they cannot process information and they need the immediacy of feedback. Or it could be that these children may have ADD or ADHD and that their impulsivity is a result of these constitutional problems. Adults, both educators and parents, need to take note of when these 'disturbances' take place to see if there is a pattern. Observational behavioural recording sheets can be helpful here.

Behaviour Record Sheet   Name: Lila   Date: _____

Time	Behaviour	Before	After
9.35	didn't come to the carpet area for storytime	was building a house from Lego	had to be brought to the carpet - was compliant
9.40	didn't answer a question which was within her capabilities	sat quietly - appeared to be listening	when focused and the question was repeated coped well
9.45	shouted out the answer to someone else's question	sat quietly - appeared to be listening	seemed to understand it wasn't her turn
9.50	wriggled and turned around to face the wall	no apparent listening to the story	when 'turned back' she looked as if she was listening
9.55	continued sitting when group stood up for the action song	looked as if she was listening	only coped with the actions from following the others
10.00	stood in the centre of the room and didn't go to her table	looked as if she was listening	when individually told what to do she complied

The adults in the early years setting were becoming concerned about Lila's apparent problems when given instructions etc. She was felt to be coping with the language areas and she gave the impression of being 'bright'. For a week the nursery nurse was asked to observe Lila's behaviours twice a day, one from 9.30 - 10.00 in the morning when it was usually a group activity such as storytime and the other from 2.00 - 2.30 in the afternoon when there were a variety of activities to choose from. It was decided that a note should be made every five minutes.

After the week's observation the profile was discussed and it was agreed that Lila seemed to have great problems focusing on tasks which were dependent on her auditory memory skills but that when supported she was quite capable of understanding and coping with all that was asked of her. Lila seemed to find visual and manual activities more satisfying. Discussions with Lila's mother showed that similar observations had been noted at home. Appropriate support and activities to help her were put in place.

Behaviour Record Sheet   Name: Denise   Date: _____

Time	Behaviour	Before	After
9.35	didn't come to the carpet area for storytime	was fiddling with another child's model	had to be brought to the carpet - wriggled and shuffled to the back of the group
9.40	pulled on another child's hair	no apparent listening to the story - looking everywhere	was moved to sit away from the other child
9.45	stood up	had wriggled to the back of the group	was moved to sit beside Mrs. P--- complained loudly
9.50	rushed around and bumped into others	group was given some actions to do from the story	wouldn't stop - had to hold Mrs. P---'s hand - complained
9.55	shouted	group was sitting on the carpet listening to instructions	taken from the group by student helper
10.00	played a car game with the helper	asked to organise this game	continued well

The adults in the early years setting were becoming concerned about Denise's behaviour especially when she was with others. As for Lila, the nursery nurse was asked to observe Denise's behaviours twice a day, at the same times. (It should be mentioned that these two children were in different settings).

After the week's observation the profile was discussed and it was agreed that Denise showed signs of impulsivity, restlessness and problems with co-operative play although she coped better on an individual basis with adults. Denise's mother said that Denise was 'wilful' and 'naughty' at home. It was agreed to monitor Denise's behaviours carefully and to put a behaviour plan in place which also would be followed in the home. If after a set amount of time Denise's behaviour continued to be inappropriate further advice would be requested to explore whether she might have ADHD or other behavioural problems.

Phonological awareness

Phonological awareness uses all the above memory skills and, as already noted in Chapter 1, poor phonological skills can be part of the specific learning difficulties profile. Phonological awareness is the understanding of sound patterns in language and the ability to use these orally. It concerns alliteration and rhyme, syllable beating, clapping a rhythm and segmentation of words. It requires children to repeat multi-syllabic words, to blend segmented heard sounds into whole words or from onset and rime, to understand analogies between words (how words can be changed to another one by altering more than one letter) and to hear the 'odd one out' from a group of rhyming words. Competence in phonological awareness is necessary for decoding and encoding words into sounds and sounds into words for reading and spelling. It is at the heart of literacy.

Motor skills

If children are going to be able to write they will need competent fine motor skills. Writing is linked with visual skills as it is a visuo-motor process. Laterality is sometimes felt to be an issue with children with specific learning difficulties.

As with visual and auditory skills all observations can occur during the day-by-day organisation of the settings rather than setting up any more formalised assessments. Again it has to be remembered that some apparent difficulties can be maturational and developmental so observations should take place over time.

Visual-motor processing

This is the ability to produce, usually in writing, what is seen. It requires a competent visual memory plus the other visual skills mentioned above. Young children experiment with paint and do not make many representational drawings or paintings at a young age. As they grow older their attempts become more understandable, with people represented by huge round heads and stick arms and legs protruding from these. Details are added as the children become more aware of what they see and recall. Similarly their first attempt at writing is scribbling where there are no recognisable letter shapes. As their attention is drawn to letter formation and as more formalised teaching occurs they begin to recall the first letter of their name and then others until they possess a small word bank of known words.

27

Fine motor control

In order to write children need to control a pencil. However, there are other activities which require competent hand-eye motor control. These are areas such as threading beads on string, fitting jigsaw puzzle clues together, using Sticklebricks, Duplo and Lego, tying shoelaces, doing up buttons, using scissors. The child who has problems with such activities will most probably have problems with pencil control as well.

Some of these children may also have gross motor control problems which can be observed when they throw, catch or kick a ball, run or hop or skip, stand on one leg, and walk up or down stairs. If children are felt to have significant gross motor skill problems then it may be necessary to alert the occupational therapy service for advice. Parents can give information about their children's development where crawling and walking were concerned as some educationists state that children with specific learning difficulties do not learn to crawl. They can also give information on whether their children seem clumsy in that they often bump into things or fall over.

Laterality and handedness

Some children take some time to decide which hand they find it easiest to use. Young children can try out both hands so it is difficult to know whether they will become right or left-handed. Using both hands when they are young does not necessarily mean they are ambidextrous and it is not helpful if the adult tries to help the child 'make up its mind' or try to change the preferred hand. Some children do not finalise their preferred hand until they are well into the infant years in school and it is usually not established until 5 to 6 years of age.

The aspect of laterality is an area that is somewhat controversial within educational circles. Some educationists feel that children with specific learning difficulties often show cross-laterality which is that they can be right-handed but left-footed and left-eyed, for example, rather than being one-side dominant. These educationists feel that this cross-laterality has a bearing on visual areas, such as discrimination and sequencing, and therefore has a direct bearing on literacy acquisition. Dyspraxic children may find difficulty with 'crossing the mid-line' so activities undertaken on the right side of the body will be performed by the right hand and if there is an activity on the left side of the body the left hand will be used. If a circle is to be drawn some children may change hands to complete the task. However, there are other educationists who feel that the laterality aspect is a red herring as there are competent readers and spellers who are also cross-lateral and this has not affected their learning. As with all the factors that might be found within a child with specific learning difficulties it is worth noting whether the child is cross-lateral as part of the overall picture.

Diagnostic assessments for early identification

It is not recommended that educators within early years settings use all of these unless there is particular concern about a child's learning needs after an observational profile has been built up. They could be more helpful if used within the reception year unless stated otherwise. The Literacy Strategy and Baseline Assessments are for use in school and are built into the reception year teaching framework.

British Picture Vocabulary Scale (BPVS) – NFER-Nelson

This is a type of achievement test which has been designed to measure receptive language understanding, the vocabulary understood and acquired. It can be administered by teachers. It is not an intelligence test as it only measures one aspect of cognitive abilities. It contains a booklet with pages of pictures, four per page. The adult gives the stimulus word and the child points to the picture this represents and the responses are recorded on sheets. There is a scoring manual which requires knowledge of the child's age and scores are given as standardised score equivalents, percentile rankings and age equivalents. Early words are nouns whilst for adults there are instances of difficult vocabulary, with the addition of adjectives, adverbs and concepts. The test has been designed to start at around 3 years and because there is no need for expressive responses it is an easy test to administer and takes a short time, especially with younger children. It is one that does not put the child under any stress. Because of the choice of four pictures there can be an element of guesswork.

Dyslexia Early Screening Test (DEST) – Nicholson and Fawcett, The Psychological Corporation

This battery of ten sub-tests has been devised as suitable for children aged from 4.6 years to 6.6 years and the assessment takes about 30 minutes to administer. The sub-tests look at some phonological aspects such as the detection of rhymes, auditory discrimination and short-term auditory memory. There is also a test called 'rapid naming' where the child has to name 20 common objects reproduced twice as pictures as quickly as possible. This works on memory retrieval skills at speed. It also assesses if the child

29

knows the names of some letters and some numbers. Fine motor skills and visual-motor skills are observed with some threading of beads and copying shapes, and postural stability is also assessed. The postural stability test is given because of the research that has been undertaken which has found that dyslexic children have slight abnormalities within the cerebellum which is the part of the brain involved in motor skill, balance and control of eye movements. However, some educationists are uneasy about this sub-test because it requires the child to be slightly 'pushed' while blindfolded. It is recommended that parents are aware of the significance of this assessment. The results can generate an 'at risk' quotient. The 'at risk' quotient can alert those working with children who appear slow at acquiring certain skills or whose progress is uneven that they might have specific literacy difficulties as they grow older. It must be emphasised that screening programmes cannot stand alone but need intervention activities which focus on the areas of difficulty.

This battery of assessments matches part of the required evidence of the *Code of Practice*, 1994, which requests evidence about clumsiness, visual sequencing and visual perception problems and weaknesses in working memory.

The Cognitive Profiling System (CoPs 1)

This series of sub-tests is suitable for children between 4 years and 8 years. The tests are computer-based and can be built in to the observational techniques within the educational settings. There are two sets, one visual and the other auditory, and the results are recorded on grids which can indicate if the child has difficulties in either the visual or auditory side or whether they have particular problems in specific sub-areas. Because the tests have a timed element built in it is important that the child can cope with mouse skills adequately. The whole test is designed to take about 45 minutes to administer and it is helpful if an adult observes how the children approach each task and to keep them on task. The tests do not have to be given in any particular order and there can be time intervals between them.

The National Foundation Baseline Scheme – NFER-Nelson

Baseline Assessment is part of the reception teacher's observational battery but this is very general and gives only an indication of possible problems. There is also an extended Baseline which can be given if the child scores particularly low on the original assessment chart. The framework has been devised for observing children during their first half term in the reception year. Many LEAs and schools have originated their own baseline assessment.

Early Years Easy Screen (EYES) – NFER-Nelson
This is an informal structured method of identifying and recording the children's development during the first six months in school. It can assess children between the ages of 4 and 5. It provides detailed follow-up activities in order to help children achieve competence in key skill areas. There is a short form to this assessment procedure.

Signpost: Baseline Assessment for the Primary Phase – NFER-Nelson
This assessment procedure is for children entering the reception class at compulsory school age and it evaluates the outcomes of the children's education within the nursery.

Climbing Frames: A Framework for Learning from Birth to Five – NFER-Nelson
This helps to plan and assess the learning of pre-school children.

The Portage Early Education Programme – NFER-Nelson
This assessment battery helps to assess and monitor children's skills. It also sets teaching goals through an individual programme of planned activities. This is often used with children with quite severe special needs but it can be useful for more moderate problems.

Building Blocks – NFER-Nelson
This incorporates three assessments. One is the LARR Test of Immergent Literacy which assesses the child's knowledge of the conventions in reading and writing English on entry to school and diagnoses strengths and needs. Another is the Early Mathematics Concepts which identifies problems within the numeracy area. The third is a reasoning assessment, Foundations for Learning. This battery can be used for children aged 4 to 5.3 years.

The National Literacy Strategy – DfEE
This is set in place in the reception year and continues throughout the child's primary school life and into the secondary. There is a framework of knowledge, of teaching objectives, which are to be taught and acquired by all pupils. In some authorities, because children enter the reception year at

the beginning of different terms depending upon their ages, the framework is set out for the whole year rather than in terms. Thus the older child who has three terms in reception can gain extra from repetition and consolidation. There are three strands to the work – word level, sentence level and text level. Phonological awareness, phonics and spelling, word recognition, graphic knowledge and spelling, vocabulary extension and handwriting are the four areas within word level work. These lend themselves to observational recording as there are set out targets which should be reached by the end of the reception year, for example the 45 high-frequency words for reading; alphabetic knowledge of both names and basic sounds; and work on phonological awareness, which includes rhyme, sound analogies, and onset and rime. Sentence level work and text level work link with expressive and receptive language areas, look at concepts of print and make the initial start to independence in reading and writing.

Chapter 3
Developing programmes and activities to meet the needs of children with specific learning difficulties

Curriculum guidance for the foundation stage (QCA/DfEE, May 2000) is a document produced to give 'stepping stones' of progress which indicate the knowledge, skills, understandings and attitudes that children need to learn during the Foundation Stage in order to achieve the early learning goals. They are not age-related and although they are set out hierarchically they need not be sequential. It is expected that:

'Practitioners must be able to observe and respond appropriately to children, informed by a knowledge of how children develop and learn and a clear understanding of possible next steps in their development and learning.'
(*Curriculum guidance for the foundation stage*, QCA/DfEE, May 2000)

The detailed guidance is given on both learning and teaching which should effectively help educators in early years settings in the planning and teaching of an appropriate curriculum within six broad areas which are:

- personal, social and emotional development;
- communication, language and literacy;
- mathematical development;
- knowledge and understanding of the world;
- physical development;
- creative development.

The guidance mentions that children have varying needs and that some children will have special educational needs and disabilities. It does not detail these but, from the aims set out on pages 8 and 9, certain aspects of how these can be linked with children and specific learning difficulties can be set out. By doing so it can be seen that observing children's strengths and weaknesses and planning appropriately for specific learning difficulties, problems need not occur in an educational vacuum but can be linked within the curricular aims of any educational setting.

The aims taken from the guidance are to support future learning by 'supporting, fostering, promoting and developing children's':

- *personal, social and emotional well-being*
  If children begin to realise at an early stage that they have learning problems compared with their peers they will not attain a strong self-image and self-esteem and, unfortunately, failure begets failure.

- *positive attitudes and dispositions towards their learning*
  This links with the above as children who find it more difficult to learn need their enthusiasms and confidences enhanced and boosted.

- *social skills*
  Co-operation with peers in learning new tasks is of prime importance.

- *attention skills and persistence*
  Children with specific learning difficulties often have attention problems and they need to learn to concentrate on their own play or on group tasks in order to gain the maximum from the learning situation.

- *language and communication*
  It is most important for all children to be given the opportunities to talk and communicate in a wide range of situations, both to adults and to their peers. In order to extend the range of their vocabulary and communication skills they need to practise and hear good modelling and they need to listen carefully. It is this area that will form a strong base for future literacy skills and an area where some children with specific learning difficulties have great problems. As the guidance says on page 45, 'The development and use of communication and language is at the heart of young children's learning.'

- *reading and writing*
  Following on from increasing competencies in language skills, children need the opportunities 'to explore, enjoy, learn about and use words and text in a broad range of contexts and to experience a rich variety of books'. Even if children in early years settings do not 'read' they need all the early reading experiences to give them a firm footing.

- *mathematics*

  As with reading and writing children need the opportunities 'to develop their understanding of number, measurement, pattern, shape and space' by the early years educators 'providing a broad range of contexts in which they can explore, enjoy, learn, practise and talk about them.'

- *knowledge and understanding of the world*

  Here some of the children with specific learning difficulties will show their strengths by being well able 'to solve problems, make decisions, experiment, predict, plan and question in a variety of contexts, and to explore and find out about their environment and people and places that have significance in their lives.' Their educators will be able to match their understanding against their possible literacy problems and note the differences.

- *physical development*

  If children are dyspraxic they will need all the opportunities provided which will help to develop and practise their fine and gross motor skills.

- *creative development*

  Some children with specific learning difficulties have strengths creatively and can draw and design competently. Others can cope well with technology. Those with problems where rhythm is concerned will find parts of music and dance difficult and some children on the ASD continuum will have difficulties with imaginative and role play activities. But all the children need these varied opportunities.

As with observation, programmes and activities to meet the needs of children with suspected specific learning difficulties should arise from the normal curriculum activities. The guidance gives a full range of suggestions and these will be noted where they pertain to specific children's needs. The headings will follow those in Chapter 2 but areas will not be subdivided in as much detail. In order to discuss some of the other specific learning difficulties there will be additional areas. There will be ideas for activities that will overlap the areas given above and early years educators will need to see which are the most relevant for the child or group of children with whom they are working.

Language and general understanding

In the guidance, language and general understanding are within the heading 'Communication, language and literacy'. It suggests that communication and language are developed through planned activities in all areas of learning and that 'time and opportunities to develop spoken language through conversations' are provided. Children should have opportunities to speak and listen whilst adults within the early years settings should value talk and help children 'to develop language for communication through interaction and expression' whilst they themselves would model the use of language.

If a child is felt to be finding the understanding and acquisition of language difficult then the following should form part of the early years activities. Sometimes these can take place as group procedures and at others these might be best carried out individually with one of the adults. These are in addition to the normal language activities and within the early years settings many of these will be already in place.

Suggestions

1. Build up names of familiar objects, nouns, which are unknown by direct instruction. Take care not to expect too many to be learnt at a time. Use 'sets' of names such as animals, transport, kitchen utensils, clothes, parts of the body etc. Check in familiar surroundings so that part of the room can become a bedroom or a shop. Large pictures or models can be used. Picture books, Big Books and other story books lend themselves to receptive and expressive language work. So does watching television or videos and it is much better for these to be shared with adults rather than children just watching the visual activities on the screen. Let the parent know so that consolidation can take place at home. Revisit the object the next day and at various times over the following weeks. Start with receptive language so that the child has to find the object and then go on to expressive language and the child giving the correct word.

2. Build up the acquisition of adjectives, adverbs, prepositions, verbs and other parts of speech in the same way. There can be a colour corner a week with different shades so that children begin to understand concepts of 'light' and 'dark' or 'shiny' or 'dull' and they can fetch objects with a particular colour. Much work can be given on prepositions where children learn one that is unknown and undertake a task that

shows they have understood and consolidated the word which then leads on to saying where the object is. Give the children a choice at first such as 'Is the cat climbing up or down the tree?' Active work in the playground or hall can be given for adverbs such as 'run swiftly' means 'run quickly' etc.

3. Help with misunderstandings where vocabulary is concerned. When words have two meanings it might be assumed that the child can understand the difference. There are mathematical words which come into this category such as 'eight/ate' and 'one/won' and even 'read/red' sounds the same. Sentences can be given such as 'the dog ate eight bones', 'Sunil won one bar of chocolate' and 'Mrs Baker read a story about a red bird' and the children can explain what these sentences are about. Then if words are used in everyday activities which might be confusing they can be dealt with similarly.

4. Help with the use of the correct tense. Young children should not be 'corrected' if they use the present tense rather than the past, for example. Here the adult can repeat the sentence using the correct tense, therefore acting as a model. If a child says 'My mum take me to the shop after playgroup and buy me this car' the adult can say 'Oh, your mum took you to the shop and bought you a car, did she?'

5. If articulation is an issue and advice has been obtained from speech and language therapists then adults can carry out any of the activities, either as a planned programme or incidentally. If advice has not been obtained and the children's articulation is weak then, wherever possible, the adult should repeat the sentences so that these are available to everyone and the children know that their messages are making sense.

6. For all children but especially for the shy and reserved child there needs to be time built in to the day for some individual conversation. Adults need to gain the confidence of the child and should not force the pace or amount of talk, but wherever possible they can move the conversation on and ask questions.

7. Within all the language activities the adult should use both closed and open questions. Closed questions will check particular areas of understanding because the answer required will need to be correct and closed questions can link with knowledge of vocabulary, (see above).

Open questions require the children to think of reasons for their answers and to give their own ideas. Even everyday activities such as the weather calendar which is changed daily can require justification. Children are asked questions such as 'what is the weather like outside?' and after the response the question can come 'what pictures shall we stick on the calendar?', 'why are we going to use this one?' The book reading session is a natural vehicle for questioning but the adult must take care not to over-question and then lose the interest of the story. As mentioned above television and video watching can also be used.

8. If children seem to have poor auditory memories and concentration adults should focus their attention by using their names before asking the question or giving the instruction. Another way of focusing attention could be to stand in front of the child and face them or even gently move their heads to face the speaker. Adults must be sure that the child will not react adversely to this kind of touch.

9. If children seem to have poor auditory memories then games can be played which help them store more than one item. These will link with the phonological awareness activities. Children's versions of 'I packed my bag' can be played, for example. Children should also be asked to repeat what they have been asked to do to make sure they have internalised this.

10. Other listening activities can be given in the form of listening to sentences. The adult says short sentences such as 'It is raining', 'I am wearing a red cardigan' and 'You have two heads' and the child has to say if the sentence is true or not true. Following on from these, use sentences that contain deliberate mistakes. The children are told to listen to the silly sentence such as 'The car skipped along the road' or 'Jea turned on the television to make a pot of tea' and they have to say what is silly about it. They can also be asked to make it a sensible sentence.

11. Expressive language has been shown to employ seven types of strategies which start from 'self-maintaining,' which is the language needed to cope with physical needs and wants, and extends to 'imagining' where imaginary situations based on real life, fantasy and original stories are developed. Many young children use 'self-maintenance', 'directing' and 'reporting' and find it harder to cope with 'towards

logical reasoning' and 'predicting' which occur when open questions are given. Others are able orally and expressively and can use 'projecting' which is empathetic, understanding others' feelings etc. and 'imagining'. Adults should be aware of the probable stage the child is coping with and try to move them forward. As has been mentioned in Chapter 2 some children with specific learning difficulties can have high levels of expressive language. However, as was also stated, if there is great concern about a child's awareness and use of language, especially in the social communication and imaginative thought areas coupled with additional problems with social relationships, then advice should be requested from those with expertise in this area because there might be problems with the ASD continuum.

12. Story language is needed to be understood and this is part of the expected text level work for the reception year in the National Literacy Strategy framework. Children are expected to be aware of some of the formal beginnings of books such as 'Once upon a time' and to be able to retell stories using some conventional speech patterns. When books are shared or when the adult makes up stories they can repeat the patterns of speech and sometimes start the phrase and see if the children can continue them correctly.

Visual areas

Competence in the visual areas are sub-skills of later literacy and numeracy acquisition. Because children acquire such skills at different times all activities etc. will need to be revisited to see whether any problems within the areas might have been due to developmental processes. Sometimes the following suggestions can occur incidentally and sometimes they may need to be set up with one particular activity for a group of children or for an individual.

Suggestions
1. If children seem to have problems with their perception, the way they look carefully at objects etc. then activities may have to be set up. A familiar toy, for example, can be described so that all details are given. When picture books are shared or when stories are read and the accompanying pictures discussed, the children should be asked to tell what they can see. Pictures can be revealed gradually and the children encouraged to guess what the whole object, picture etc. would be.

2. More detailed activities can be organised. There are many books that encourage children to see hidden objects, for example saucepans are 'hidden' in trees or there might be a picture of a kitchen with a bed in it. They have to look very deliberately and find things that might not be expected. A dog might have six legs so the child has to know the number of legs a dog should have and then tell what is silly. There are packs of cards that contain pictures of everyday objects which have something incorrect about them and the child has to determine what this is.

3. As has been pointed out in Chapters 1 and 2 some children seem to prefer coloured backgrounds to pages in books so they reject books with white pages. This may be because of Irlen Syndrome and apart from requesting advice from others, children with this problem may be helped by giving them coloured backgrounds, even photocopying print onto coloured paper, or by being supplied with particular coloured overlays which will make looking at print easier and more comfortable.

4. For supporting those children with visual discrimination problems there are many workbooks that contain rows of objects which are mostly similar but one is slightly different. There may be teddy bears with scarves and one will not have a scarf and the child has to find the different one. These are graded in difficulty with the more demanding pictures shown of shapes with one which is only slightly different.

5. Visual discrimination activities can take place out of the early years setting where adults can encourage the child to look carefully at the houses, the shops, the cars, to look at colours and shapes etc. If the words 'same' and 'different' are known these can be built into the activities.

6. When letters and numbers are introduced this can be done in two ways. One is by using the written form such as a brightly coloured alphabet frieze or number line or being introduced to letters and numbers in books. The other way is using three-dimensional letters and numbers which can be held. Magnetic letters and numbers are often in evidence in children's homes, often attached to refrigerators, and wooden or plastic letters are used in educational settings. Although letters and numbers that can be held and used are most

useful the adult working with the child must be aware that there are those that can become something else if turned upside down or back to front. Children need to learn that letters have a fixed position in space. As the children grow more aware of the visual arrangement of letters they have to learn to 'read' and 'write' them correctly. However, it is important to remember that confusion of similar letters is a normal occurrence.

7. Story sequencing cards is a helpful activity where the child is given a set of pictures that tell a story as long as they are placed in the correct order. This activity can be linked with expressive language as the child has to tell the story using the picture clues. Stories such as *The Very Hungry Caterpillar* uses a strong sequence.

8. As children become better readers and spellers they have to learn how to see letters and words in sequence and to remember them.

9. Work on sets of objects where children find things of the same shape or colour or objects that are used in the kitchen or in the garage, for example, can form the basis for visual categorisation. Children can be given pictures to sort. These can be into colour, shapes, sizes or other categories. As reading and spelling progress children find similarities and differences between letters and words.

10. There are many games which can be played to help visual memory skills. Adults can ask particular questions about pictures they have shown or about something that happened in Assembly. They can set up another adult to stand in front of the children for a length of time and then that adult leaves. The children are then asked about the colour of the adult's clothes, whether the adult was carrying anything and what it was, and many other details. The children might have been warned that they had to look carefully. This can also be done with television and video watching. Too often young children watch television or videos without taking in detail. Although they gather an overall impression they cannot recall colours that someone was wearing, an animal that appeared, for example. Pictures can be shown and talked about. Then the picture is covered and questions asked in order to see what details the children have picked up. Simple Kim's Game can be laid out. A tray of objects is laid out and after the children have looked at it for some short time it is covered and they name the

objects. Another version is to set up the objects but after a short time the children shut their eyes. Two or three objects are removed and the children have to remember what these are.

11. Games such as picture snap are useful so that children have to remember what picture was on a particular card. This leads on to letters and words later. Other games such as pairs or Pelmanism lead on to memory skills enhancement, with pictures first and then words and letters. Pelmanism is a memory game which can be played with picture cards, playing cards or cards with colours, symbols, letters or words on them. The cards are placed face downwards on the table and one player turns over two at a time. If a pair is shown the player wins it. If dissimilar cards are turned over these are replaced face downward in the same position. Young children should start with few cards with either colours or pictures and as their memories increase so should the number of cards. Dominoes help with visual sequencing and here there is a link with numeracy. Lotto with pictures and symbols can also be helpful. Visual sequencing and visual memory can be worked on with cards with shapes drawn on them. Two cards at first are put in order. Then they are muddled and the child has to put them back in the same order. The length of the sequence can be increased as the child becomes more proficient at this activity.

12. When reading and spelling takes place the children have to recognise letter shapes and then they have to name them and supply their basic sounds. Words for reading have to be recognised as a whole shape, their 'labels' learnt and then recalled verbally. This often occurs incidentally when children realise that their teacher has used the same label when a particular shape of letters has been used. This often happens with the children's names and so these are learnt even though they might be similar in shape to others such as 'Charlotte, Charlie, Christine, Chloe and Christopher'. Words for spelling have also to be remembered as a whole shape, with the letters in the correct sequence and then written from memory.

The guidance for the Foundation Stage gives more advice about the skills needed for mathematical development than it does for early reading and spelling skills. Where visual skills are concerned it mentions sorting, matching, seeking patterns, making connections, recognising relationships and working with numbers, shapes, space and measures. It states that shape awareness would involve 'recognising similarities and differences and distinguishing properties of shape'. The activities mentioned above can have patterns and shapes added to them if it is felt that children need extra mathematical activities.

Auditory areas

Competence in the auditory areas are also sub-skills of later literacy and numeracy acquisition. As with visual skills, because children acquire such skills at different times all activities etc. will need to be revisited to see whether any problems within the areas might have been due to developmental processes. Sometimes the following suggestions can occur incidentally and sometimes they may need to be set up with one particular activity for a group of children or for an individual.

Suggestions

1. If it is felt that a child has 'selective hearing' in that they choose when they want to hear and react this will be noted by the adults within particular circumstances. If there is a pattern to their apparent loss of hearing then it might be the activity presented or the activity in which they are involved that will need targeting. Children can be observed in everyday activities especially when they have to follow instructions as in PE and Assembly time.

2. If children have to be focused into listening the adult should make eye contact or use their names before asking the question or giving the information or instruction.

3. Children can be asked to be very quiet and to listen very carefully. Then a list of sounds from inside and/or outside the building can be given.

4. Tapes with familiar, or even unfamiliar, sounds can be played so the children have to work out what they are hearing. To make this easier pictures could be supplied so that the children match the sound with the picture.

5. In order to hear differences in sounds musical activities relating to high and low sounds, loud or soft instruments, single sounds or more than one could be organised.

43

6. The game 'Simon Says' encourages careful listening and children can at first be asked to carry out a simple instruction such as 'Simon says clap your hands' and then more than one instruction such as 'Simon says touch your nose and your shoes'. This also helps sequential listening.

7. To encourage children to listen carefully to words the children are asked to listen carefully for a particular type of word (such as a number, name, colour, animal etc.) from four words spoken by the adult. When they hear the word they indicate by putting up their hands. If it was an animal the words could be 'tree, picnic, elephant, sausage'.

8. In order to read and spell well auditory sequencing is necessary. Sentences are usually said in the correct order. Short ones can be made up with one word out of place and the children have to work out what it should be, such as 'Ben's dog ran down the road busy'.

9. Guessing what comes next in a sentence will help later contextual reading. 'Mr Potts drove a big black ...' and the children can make several suggestions such as 'lorry/van/train/car/dumper truck'. After ends of sentences, missing other words out can be tried such as prepositions and here there is a link with expressive and receptive language.

10. Often children need to know their house number, their birthdates, their brothers' and sisters' names, their telephone numbers, and later the days of the week and the months of the year in sequence. Alphabetical order also is required as the child moves into the reception year. Starting with two digits or two words or two letters the children can repeat a sequence and build on those until they acquire the requisite skill. This activity has a link with auditory memory.

11. Nursery rhymes and songs can be taught and learnt so that the words are in the correct order. Songs like 'Ten green bottles' are particularly useful. The alphabet sequence is often taught similarly and there appear to be two tunes with one requiring the 'lmnop' to be sung rapidly so many children muddle these letters. Appearing to be able to sing the alphabet does not ensure that children can say it – but it is a start.

12. When children play with words they need to be able to categorise them. Sets are used for early numeracy activities. With auditory skills sets are made of words starting with the same letter or ending with the same sound. These activities link with auditory discrimination as the children need to be able to hear and understand the difference between words and with phonological awareness where games on rhyme are given.

13. Because so many of life's responses are given auditorially, auditory memory skills are most important. Children can neglect these skills, especially if they treat visual/auditory experiences as more a seeing activity than a hearing activity. This can happen when watching television as the strong visual images prevail over the sound, which in the case of speech can be quite fast. When watching television children should be encouraged to listen so that they can answer particular questions.

14. Learning songs, nursery rhymes, jingles and poems require auditory memory skills and using actions can add to the memory process.

15. Learning important facts such as addresses, telephone numbers, birthdays, names of the family and names of other children may have to be directly taught and rehearsed. There can be charts for these in the early years setting and the children can gain stickers or other rewards when they have remembered certain information. As they become more proficient days of the week, months of the year and the alphabet can be checked in this way. Here the link with auditory sequencing is the auditory sequential memory.

16. When sharing books etc. the adult can ask particular questions, especially to see if the children can recall particular details from the text, quoting the text, rather than just generalising.

17. Messages can be given to children to remember. Short ones at first where they take the message to another adult in the setting. These can be increased in time and intervals between the remembering and the delivering can be built into the activity.

Phonological awareness

Because phonological awareness is most important where later reading and spelling are concerned the activities here will form a section of their own. However, as has been stated previously phonological awareness uses all the above memory skills. There are activities that can be given as class or group work but some may need to be tailored to the individual child, particularly in the reception class. There is no suggested order for these activities but some appear to be more difficult for younger children, such as phoneme deletion and analogies. All these activities are auditory and require competent listening skills and the ability to respond either orally or using some kind of action.

Suggestions

1. Clapping a rhythm in the music lesson can start to make children aware of the beats within words. Use tunes with strong beats to start with which do not require too many fast claps. Use musical instruments that can be beaten in rhythm such as drums, tambourines or shakers such as dried peas in a box. Skipping and marching to a strong beat will also help.

2. Working on rhythm will be a link with syllable beating. First there can be clapping the beats in the children's names with the adult modelling at first. Next the children will clap and count the beats simultaneously. Then the next stage is clapping and counting other words. One beat words can cause problems as children often want to split these into two such as 'bo-ox' for 'box' and 'ch-air' for 'chair'. This type of problem occurs if they work on onset and rime activities before understanding about syllable breaks. Some children find it hard to count and clap/beat at the same time. They may beat the correct number of syllables but give the incorrect number. The adult should be ready to help here.

3. When the children are secure at beating they can say the word in its syllables. Children will enjoy finding long words. Because this is playing orally with words the adult can supply some nonsense words which entails the children being able to hold onto an unknown set of sounds and work on them. Children can also produce their own nonsense words.

4. Nonsense words and real words can be used for repetition by the child. Short words can be given such as 'pelp' or 'night' and then other syllables added such as 'pelping' or 'nightgown'. Once children can repeat shorter words three or four syllable words can be supplied.

46

5. Oral work on initial sounds is important where the children have to be able to hear a word and the sound it begins with. This can be played as 'I spy'. For quite young children before this game is played with sounds it can be played as colours so the adult says 'I spy with my little eye something that is yellow'. This will introduce the concept of the game. If children have problems discriminating sounds they will find this activity difficult and the adult may have to emphasise the initial sound. However, care must be taken not to voice the initial sound, which is usually a single consonant at first, or the children will start learning that a 't' is a 'tuh' for example. As the children become more proficient the game can be made slightly more demanding so that the adult will say 'I spy with my little eye something beginning with the same sound as "window".' The children have to take off this sound and then find 'wall' or 'white' or 'wheel'.

6. Oral lists of words can be made such as all the words starting with 'm' as in 'mummy/mouse/me/music'. This could be an elimination game with children standing up and taking it in turns to give a word. If they cannot, or get a word incorrect, they have to sit down. Of course, care has to be taken here that the same child does not always sit down first and the adult will have to judge when to give clues and when to help.

7. Once children can think of words connected to their initial sounds the adult can turn the activity around and give words and ask if they begin with a particular sound. The children have to hear the word, remember the word, take off the sound, connect it to the sound given and decide whether this is correct or not. For example, the adult might say 'does window begin with "w"?' or 'does goat begin with "c"?' Children with weak auditory discrimination or weak memory skills may find this activity challenging.

8. To help auditory memory skills two or three words with the same letter sound and one that is different can be given as in 'nut, table, nose' and the child has to pick the 'odd one out'.

9. As children grow more proficient at initial sounds then similar activities using end and medial sounds can be given. This is quite a sophisticated activity.

10. Working on rhyme provides many activities. It has already been mentioned that children are given nursery rhymes etc. to sing and remember but unless they have a 'feel' for words and automatically appear aware that certain words sound the same, e.g. 'Humpty' and 'Dumpty' and 'wall' and 'fall', they will need this emphasised. When such rhyming songs and poems are given the adult can stress the rhyming words just to give an initial indication that these words are similar.

11. To gain the children's awareness of the rhyme pattern the adult can change the rhyming word to another or ask the children to guess what it might be. In the nursery rhyme just mentioned the second line could become 'Humpty Dumpty looked like a ...?' and the adult can make the shape of a 'ball' if the children cannot guess. Another line could be 'Humpty Dumpty was wrapped in a ...?' Given the words 'wall/fall/ball/shawl' the children can be asked if they can hear anything interesting about these words and when someone says they sound the same the children can be asked if they can think of other words which can be linked with these.

12. Rhyming activities such as supplying a rhyming word to a given stimulus word, making up nonsense rhyming words, finding a rhyming word for children's names (but care must be taken here), making up little poems with the adult's help are all ways of enabling the children to link words with the same sound. Because this is oral work it does not matter if the words are visually different.

13. As an alternative to the 'listening carefully to words' activity mentioned earlier the children are again asked to listen carefully for a particular type of word (such as a number, name, colour, animal etc.) from four words spoken by the adult. This time all the words rhyme. If the category was a colour, sequences could be 'seen, queen, green, lean' or 'quack, black, stack, shack'.

14. When children are secure at understanding the concept of rhyme they can be asked to find the 'odd one out' in a list of three or four given rhyming words such as 'pen, when, stop, then'.

15. Before children are able to blend words for themselves when reading they need to know what blending is about. Adults can say words in

their component parts in either robotic or whispered voices and the children have to say the whole word. Nonsense or real words can be used and both sound by sound, phoneme by phoneme, or onset and rime can be worked on. Examples of these are 'sh-o-p' or 'sh-op'.

16. As children become more competent with aural/oral work on words they need to understand analogies which is how words can be connected. Syllable or phoneme deletion can be worked on. A word is supplied and the child is asked what is left if the initial syllable or sound is removed, e.g. 'the word is "window", what is left if the "win" is taken away?' or 'the word is "table", what is left if the "t" is taken away?' More complicated work on this is the end syllable or sound or even medial sounds. Work can also be given on how words can be changed to others by altering one or more sounds. Here the word could be 'hand' and the child has to remove the first sound and use an 's' to make 'sand'.

Phonological activities for the reception year in the National Literacy Strategy word level work include working with rhymes, generating new words by analogy, hearing and identifying initial and final sounds in words, understanding alphabetical order, identifying alliteration and working on onsets and rimes in speech. Some of the above activities can form part of the oral early literacy skills within the early years settings whilst others will link with the more 'formalised' learning within the reception class.

Motor skills

Dyspraxic pupils and others with specific learning difficulties may have poor gross motor skills; they may have poor fine motor skills or a combination of the two. For later writing they will need competent fine motor skills which is linked with competent visual skills. Most children enjoy picking up coloured crayons, pencils and felt-tip pens and making marks on paper which to them is 'writing'. This should be encouraged.

Activities to help pupils with gross motor skill problems can occur in PE and games lessons and in other activities that need more global movements. Unless a child has had an assessment and a set programme of activities from an occupational therapist, adults can use the normal teaching situations to support the so-called 'clumsy' child. Only a few ideas will be listed in this area because there are books on dyspraxia which can be most useful. These are listed in the appendices. All gross movements and activities supporting these should be broken down into their component parts. Fine motor skills activities take place as a day-by-day occurrence but where writing skills are found to be lacking the child may need some individual support.

Gross motor activities

1. Games such as 'Simon Says' are useful because the child has to follow instructions. In the playground there can be games set up like 'The ally ally O', 'Oranges and Lemons', 'Ring-a-ring-a-roses' where there is sequence and movement but where the children can follow each other's example. Any 'follow-my-leader' game is useful. 'The Hokey-Cokey' involves actions with parts of the body and there are many songs that require actions.

2. When children are running freely adults can see which ones bump into each other because they have problems with their position in space. Activities can be set up so that children have to walk and then run around objects without touching them and then other children can become 'trees' and particular children have to explore the 'forest' without bumping into a tree.

3. Because skipping, hopping, jumping and balancing can be difficult activities for some children these should be given extra practice and as much adult support as is necessary. Balancing on one leg can be a difficult skill and children should start with a support before trying to balance without any aid. Balancing on a wide strip at ground level can become a narrower strip at ground level and then a wide plank a few inches above the ground. Wobble boards can be fun for balance and box tunnels are helpful for crawling, especially if the child did not crawl when a baby. Many children find climbing frames daunting because these require coordinated arm and leg movements. Adults can support these pupils so they know they will not fall.

4. Practice with catching and throwing a ball can be started with beanbags which are floppy and then larger soft balls before smaller soft balls are used. Both hands will be used before the preferred hand, especially as many children have not established their handedness at an early age.

Fine motor control

1. Some children have problems with self-organisational skills such as dressing and undressing. Young children need velcroed shoes or pull-on slippers. Velcro instead of buttons is very handy. Knowing which is the front or back of garments can be shown by having something distinctive to differentiate these. If children have problems with putting their arms into sleeves they need clothes that are not too tight and they need much practice. Dressing a toy will give them a visual clue.

2. Help with hand-eye motor control can be given with activities such as threading items on string, playing catching fish with a hook on a line, fitting jigsaw puzzle clues together with a few pieces at first, using Sticklebricks, building bricks by making towers and playing with Duplo.

3. Cutting can occur with dough first before paper. Adults need to provide both right and left-handed scissors so that the child can choose.

4. Activities such as tying shoelaces and doing up buttons can be presented on a toy before the children have to prove they can cope with these skills independently.

5. Computers and PlayStations etc. are found in the majority of homes and early years settings. Children can practise with mouse and stick skills and often they become quite adept at this type of activity but cannot cope with pencil and paper.

Visual-motor processing

1. Painting using either their fingers or brushes is a good activity for experimentation with shape and colour and hand-eye control. At first the children tend to cover the page with different shapes and they cover these with more and more paint, often producing a mucky brown final 'picture'. If adults take the pictures away when they feel they are 'at their best' the children do not learn to use their own ideas about an end product.

2. Similarly children need to be able to practise their early drawing skills and it is only by looking carefully and using visual skills that children's drawings become recognisable. Of course, they also need some maturity in being able to control something as thin as a pencil.

3. Writing skills start by scribbling. Letter shapes are copied and within their indeterminate lines there is often a capital letter which is usually the one that begins their name. Because they see their names on their trays, their pegs, their book bags etc. they learn this one first and sometimes it takes time for them to realise that this letter also has a lower case counterpart.

4. Before learning to form letters children can be given some other pencil activities such as tracing around shapes, colouring in patterns, copying patterns, doing dot-to-dot exercises and drawing common shapes such as a circle and a square. Pencils should not be too thick because of the children's small fingers. At first they will use a fisty grip but later a correct pencil grip needs to be modelled and encouraged. If children start with a bad habit they might find it hard to lose it. Large letters and sky writing can occur first. An adult models with large arm movements how a particular letter is formed and the children copy. Sometimes it is helpful if words are also used such as 'down, up halfway and round and join' (for the letter 'b'). The adult should be facing away from the children so that they copy exactly. Therefore, another adult needs to be watching and helping the children with their arm movements.

5. Handwriting should be a taught skill with the adult modelling exactly how letters should start and finish. If children are definitely left-handed a left-handed adult might be a more appropriate model.

The guidance for the Foundation Stage under its heading 'communication, language and literacy' suggests that within the early years settings there are opportunities provided for 'children to see adults writing and for children to experiment with writing for themselves through making marks, personal writing symbols and conventional script'. The National Literacy Strategy for the reception year expects that the children should acquire a comfortable and efficient pencil grip. However, comfortable for some children means inefficiency. Also expected is that children should produce a controlled line which supports letter formation and to write letters using the correct sequence of movements.

Reading
Reading problems can be identified at quite an early stage – that is the child who cannot recall sight words, who cannot cope with phonic

decoding skills and who cannot cope independently with early readers. However, as has been emphasised within this book, it is more difficult to identify dyslexia at an early age. It might be better to accept that there will be children who, rather than having problems with learning to read, have problems learning to read at specified times in their school careers. Instead of requiring various processes and skills to be acquired at set times in a child's school life educators should work towards those targets at the child's own rate of learning. This is probably the only approach for children with dyslexia. The activities given in this chapter may be helpful for giving the children early learning skills.

Chapter 4
Working with parents

Parents are integral to 'sound' education especially where young children are concerned. Not only have they much to offer in describing their child's developmental information they also can back up and consolidate the work and learning situations that occur in the early years settings. However, partnership with parents in a true working sense does not always run smoothly. Relationships need working on and there should be trust on both sides. Educators should be responsive to any concerns that the parents might have and should take seriously the information they are able to impart. Educators must also share their concerns. Often they do not wish to worry parents at an early stage but parents require an honest and open approach. One of the problems parents have with the educational world is that often they feel they have not been kept informed at all stages.

Specific learning difficulties may not be a term in general use but other words such as 'dyslexia', 'dyspraxia', 'ADHD' and 'autism' are used in the media and parents use the information they read to label their children when they feel that there might be a learning problem. Unfortunately magazines etc. often give simplistic checklists and these fuel the parents' anxieties. For example, if articles state that because dyslexic children have a different learning style, because they often appear to be bright and quick-thinking, because they may have expressive language problems, because they show motor skills problems, because they can cope with constructional toys, because they make a slow start with reading and spelling it is important that their dyslexic problems are identified as early as possible. The children should not be allowed to fail and specialised help should be given. Parents become very worried given such information and advice. They read the checklists and note which items pertain to their own child.

Adults in the early years settings must be able to accept the parents' concerns and share these, even though they may feel that there is nothing to worry about and that any problem noticed could have a developmental basis.

Listening to parents

Parents should be welcomed into the early years setting, not only to bring and collect their children but to talk over any worries. Two-way discussion between parent and adult within the setting should aim to:

- encourage both sides to talk freely and share information etc. openly;
- communicate openly and avoid any misunderstanding;
- establish mutual respect and trust and confidence on both sides;
- acknowledge honesty;
- clarify any potential problems;
- encourage co-operation.

If a meeting has been arranged rather than being just a 'drop-in' occasion the listener needs the following in order for the discussion to flow:

- adequate preparation such as having the relevant information to hand;
- appropriate planning so that both sides know how long the meeting will last and there needs to be enough time for all points to be aired;
- a suitable room which can be comfortable and free from interruptions.

Educators need to be aware that they are often seen to be the 'experts' so they need to build up skills, both passive and active. These can be listed as:

- having a clear mind without apparent prejudice concerning the children's problems or their parents;
- being able to listen and understand, not just someone who 'hears', the development of good listening skills;
- knowing how to acknowledge parental feelings (and their own);
- coping with taking notes, either during the session if the parents do not mind, or making a résumé afterwards;
- sending a report afterwards if necessary that is jargon-free;
- being able to talk through the main points, to recap and rephrase where necessary;
- using ways to open up the conversation if the parents find it difficult to discuss and explain their concerns.

The parents' role

There are many of the observable items set out in Chapter 2 which parents will be aware of. Some of these will form their concerns which they may wish to share in the early years setting. Others they may be able to supply if the adults within the settings ask for it. Children often behave and act differently depending on where they are so shared knowledge between home and setting can be invaluable.

What is important is that parents consolidate and work on activities that complement those in the early years settings. If the rapport between parent and educator is not good, if the parent does not trust the educator or if the parent feels that other advice might be more beneficial then the child might receive mixed messages and education is hindered. It is too early at this stage of education for a child to receive private tuition.

Parents need to be aware that there is a great deal of incidental education being provided within the home situation. Gross motor skills are developed through going up and down stairs, learning to ride a tricycle and bicycle, climbing on a climbing frame, being taken to the children's playground, to games such as chase. The list is endless. Fine motor skills are helped through learning to undress and dress, helping with simple household tasks such as cooking, using the computer for games or other such educational/play toys, using scissors and painting, drawing and 'pretend' writing. More 'academic' type activities are guided through coping with pocket money, becoming aware of the passage of time, learning names, addresses and telephone numbers and being aware that letters that label food items, shops etc. can be read as words. There are so many learning activities which many parents work on without being aware of their true educational value.

Parents need to understand that learning is acquired through discovery and problem solving, trial and error, where children attempt to work things out for themselves and later achieve it. When problem solving the children come to understand and process the particular activity to be solved. They may need to have some prior knowledge in order to solve that task but once it is within their capabilities they should be able to use the existing or newly acquired knowledge within new situations. They will make analogies between the circumstances. Parents have to beware of not jumping in too soon to help. They know when frustration might occur. There is also the modelling method of learning where someone, usually older, shows a skill etc. and the children imitate and the learnt task is put into their own repertoire. Direct instruction is a teaching method where the adult imparts 'rules' of a particular skill to the child.

Within the home this method is rarely necessary except maybe for safety's sake. Direct instruction is not always a satisfactory method of teaching because when the children use this step-by-step approach, learning by rote a particular skill, they may not completely understand it. They may not understand the process or the concept (for example, learning how to add up sums over 10 when they do not really understand the concept of number).

In Chapter 3 there is mention that some of the activities can be carried out within the home. Rather than listing these again it is hoped that the early years educators will provide information for activities in the home or that they and the parents will work out together what would work best with a particular child.

Because most of the activities in this chapter were skills that worked towards competence in literacy or had some relevance to other specific learning difficulties there was not information directly given about sharing books.

Sharing books, reading with children and telling stories to children is of immense value and should start when the children are babies and carry on even when the child becomes a reader. It is important that parents carry out this activity with enjoyment and there are just a few helpful ideas which can be given. In the ideal situation, which cannot always occur because of time factors and the presence of other children who also want attention, these are:

1. Parent and child should sit comfortably side by side or the child should be on the parent's lap. Bedtime is a good time for this activity because the child can then be away from the rest of the family and the television.

2. There should be no distractions so even if the time is limited it should be just for that particular child.

3. The child should choose the book which is excellent for helping with decision making. Often the same book will be chosen time and again and sometimes the parent may need to steer the child's selection (or read two books). Although parents often remember the books they enjoyed as a child and want their child to enjoy them too this does not always happen as interests change.

4. Parent and child should discuss the pictures. Pictures are important both for helping with expressive language and with giving information about the story.

5. Parent and child should talk about the story, what has happened so far, what might happen etc.

6. The reading should be as expressive as possible with the child allowed or even encouraged to join in.

7. The parent should show pleasure and interest in the book. Remember that adult interests are more sophisticated than the child's so one might not have enjoyed the experience as much as the child has.

8. Encourage other family members to read to the child. It is important that the child does not just think that reading stories is a task which belongs to one particular family member and if possible model reading so that the child sees that as many family members as possible get enjoyment from books when they are reading to themselves.

Specific learning difficulties, dyslexia, dyspraxia or other special needs might develop as the child grows older. However, if observation has been ongoing, if the rapport between the early years setting and the home has been strong and if the activities provided have been structured, meaningful and well-delivered the basis for support will have been started and the child will have been given a firm foundation within the early years, the foundation years.

Appendices

References

Carle, E. (1970) *The Very Hungry Caterpillar.* Puffin Books: London.

DES (1978) *Special Educational Needs (The Warnock Report).* HMSO: London.

DES (1981) *Education Act 1981.* HMSO: London.

DfE (1994) *Code of Practice on the Identification and Assessment of Pupils with Special Educational Needs.* DfE: London.

DfEE (2000) *SEN Code of Practice on the Identification and Assessment of Pupils with Special Educational Needs* and the *SEN Thresholds: Good Practice Guidance on Identification and Provision for Pupils with Special Educational Needs,* Draft Code and Guidance. DfEE: London.

Dyspraxia Foundation, *Information for Parents.* The Dyspraxia Foundation: Hitchin.

Jacobson, J. (ed.) (1997) *The Dyslexia Handbook 1997.* The British Dyslexia Association: Reading.

QCA/DfEE (2000) *Curriculum Guidance for the Foundation Stage.* QCQ/DfEE: London.

Riddick, B. (1996) *Living With Dyslexia.* Routledge: London.

Smythe, I. (ed.) (2000) *The Dyslexia Handbook 2000.* The British Dyslexia Association: Reading.

Useful books

Macintyre, C. (2001) *Dyspraxia 5-11.* David Fulton Publishers: London.

Mortimer, H. (2000) *Developing Individual Behaviour Plans in Early Years.* NASEN: Tamworth.

Mortimer, H. (2000) *The Music Makers Approach: Inclusive Activities for Young Children with Special Educational Needs*. NASEN: Tamworth.

Ott, P. (1997) *How to Detect and Manage Dyslexia: A Reference and Resource Manual*. Heinemann: Oxford.

Portwood, M. (1999) *Developmental Dyspraxia Identification and Intervention: A Manual for Parents and Professionals*. Second Edition. David Fulton Publishers: London.

The Dyslexia Handbooks published yearly. The British Dyslexia Association: Reading.

Useful names and addresses

The British Dyslexia Association
98 London Road, Reading, RG1 5AU
Telephone: Helpline: 0118 966 8271
Email: info@dyslexiahelp-bda.demon.co.uk
Website: www.bda-dyslexia.org.uk

The Dyspraxia Foundation
8 West Alley, Hitchin, Herts., SG5 1EG
Telephone: 01462 455016
Helpline: 01462 454986

The National Association for Special Educational Needs
4/5 Amber Business Village, Amber Close, Amington, Tamworth, B77 4RP
Telephone: 01827 311500
Email: welcome@nasen.org.uk
Website: www.nasen.org.uk